CATCH THE WIND

Seth Pomeroy

Published by InstantPublisher
P.O. Box 340
410 Highway 72 West
Collierville, TN 38027
www.instantpublisher.com

Cover Design by InstantPublisher

To order additional copies:

Calvary Books and Gifts
1401 Calvary Road
North Little Rock, AR 72116
501-758-3090

Dedication

Never do we have a single service, ever, where Bishop Holmes does not promote the importance of praying for at least thirty minutes a day. Some well-known preachers have asked him why this church is so successful. His answer is just too simplistic for many: "Number one, prayer, number two, prayer, and number three, prayer!"

Just about all the miracles we will see are going to come through red hot, anointed, fiery prayer!

With these few words, I dedicate this book to Bishop J.N. Holmes for his endless burden to see all of us dig out our own wells of prayer. As I learned, only I can dig my well! Thanks, Bishop Holmes, for the fervency you have in every message to promote prayer in Jesus' name!

Lord bless,
Seth Pomeroy

Acknowledgements

I wish to give honor to my wonderful, God-fearing family: my wife, Linda; my daughter, Sharon, and her husband, Wade; their daughters, Tavia, Tandice and Taegan; my daughter, Kara, and her husband, Sammy; their daughters, Shayna and Alayna, and their son, Myles; my son, Seth, and his wife, Chelsea; their daughters, Mary Grace, Abigail, Jane Claire, and Charlotte.

God bless all of you!
Dad ("Popper")

I also want to express my appreciation and support of Pastor Nathan Holmes. He is an outstanding young man who is following in the footsteps of Bishop Holmes. I can't be thankful enough to see this young man guiding our youth, which includes my children and grandchildren!

I want to give credit to Zach Ward, my very capable editor and to Robyn Duty who has gone the second mile in typing this book.

Table of Contents

Foreword

James 1:22-23 *"But be ye doers of the word, and not hearers only, deceiving your own selves. For if any be a hearer of the word, and not a doer, he is like unto a man beholding his natural face in a glass:"* James 2:14 *"What doth it profit, my brethren, though a man say he hath faith, and have not works? can faith save him?*
James 5:16, *"Confess your faults one to another, and pray one for another, that ye may be healed. The **effectual fervent** prayer of a righteous man availeth much."*

These were some Scriptures that came to my mind as I started to write this foreword on behalf of my father. Through my formative years, I remember hearing him cry out to God late into the night on a consistent basis. He heard the Word of God and became a doer. You can tell how much faith a person has based on their actions or works and he has shown for decades his faith in God by his prayer life! Finally, the Bible says that the effectual fervent prayer of a righteous man availeth much. I have seen this work in my father's life for many years as we have seen many victories come about as a result of his prayer life.

Bishop Holmes has consistently preached the message of prayer for many years and my father has continued to apply the message to his life. If you pass through the sanctuary at First Pentecostal Church very many times during the day, there is a good chance that you will hear Seth Pomeroy doing what he loves best—crying out to God!

Seth T. Pomeroy

Introduction

After years of an intercessory prayer life (which did not start until 1988 even though I received the Holy Ghost in 1971), I have felt led to write a short book of parables, analogies, and thoughts of what has come to me in prayer.

Living in fiery, fervent prayer is so exciting. I have an eager, daily call to get to the church. I can promise you that it did not happen overnight! I have cultivated prayer for many years and our great Lord has honored it.

What you read in this book has come to me in prayer and God has driven me to put it on paper. Those great "ah-ha" moments have happened to me many times while in prayer and, of course, have driven me to deeper wells of anointing. I prayed that if I ever wrote anything again, it would have to be penned by the Lord.

I think many times of the parable of the ten virgins: five had the oil and five did not. These are virgins! Five were prepared for the Lord to come and, as you know, the other five did not make it on the day of the Lord's return.

This parable can be found in Matthew 25: 1-13: *"Then shall the kingdom of heaven be likened unto ten virgins, which took their lamps, and went forth to meet the bridegroom.*
And five of them were wise, and five were foolish.

*They that were foolish took their lamps, and took no oil
with them:*
But the wise took oil in their vessels with their lamps.
*While the bridegroom tarried, they all slumbered and
slept.*
*And at midnight there was a cry made, Behold, the
bridegroom cometh; go ye out to meet him.*
Then all those virgins arose, and trimmed their lamps.
*And the foolish said unto the wise, Give us of your oil;
for our lamps are gone out.*
But the wise answered, saying, Not so; *lest there be not
enough for us and you: but go ye rather to them that
sell, and buy for yourselves.*
*And while they went to buy, the bridegroom came; and
they that were ready went in with him to the marriage:
and the door was shut.*
*Afterward came also the other virgins, saying, Lord,
Lord, open to us.*
*But he answered and said, Verily I say unto you, I know
you not.*
*Watch therefore, for ye know neither the day nor the
hour wherein the Son of man cometh."*

I have burned anointed, fiery prayer into my
heart daily, which I perceive to be the "oil" in the
lamps. I want to be ready for the Heaven side of
eternity.

I hope someone can glean a little bit from these writings. I must have this oil—fiery, fervent, anointed prayer!

Lord bless,
Seth Pomeroy

CATCH THE WIND

Chapter 1
The Holy Ghost and Anointed Prayer

I remember receiving the glorious Holy Ghost in 1971. The date was June 1st at 2:00 am! After I returned from Texas to Colorado, I remember praying every night for about three weeks until I spoke in tongues as the Spirit gave the utterance. Right after receiving the Holy Ghost, Satan attempted, as usual, to remind me that I just garbled some words; however, I *knew* I had the Holy Ghost. By praying every evening for three weeks, I established the beginning of, by far, the greatest experience of my life. To this day, this has grown into a very powerful experience and is rooted with much daily, fiery, anointed prayer.

I write this chapter because I feel a necessity to do so. Over many years, I have seen the Lord fill numerous people with the Holy Ghost. Each person that receives this great gift prays with fire and is filled with excitement! That is supposed to happen! Over the years, I have noticed that some folks are gone within a period of a few weeks—very sad.

I have learned that a new convert must begin a prayer life *immediately* or the devil will rip that person apart! After I received the Holy Ghost, old friends pushed against my newfound faith; however, in my case, I was able to avoid these calls for another drink or date because I was so hungry for truth and righteousness.

The day we live in is very perilous for everyone. Drugs and alcohol of all kinds are a fingertip away and, sadly, youth pregnancies are off the chart. So I say the only way out of this world and into Heaven with peace, joy, and happiness is through receiving the Holy Ghost and *immediately* establishing a daily, anointed prayer life! I promise that will work. In the past, I had ten thousand excuses not to pray, but starting in 1988, I butted heads with the devil and, of course, my own flesh, until the fire came down!

Daily, anointed prayer is as essential to the Lord and our soul as food, oxygen, and other daily needs are to our very existence!

Acts 2:38 says, *"Then Peter said unto them, Repent, and be baptized every one of you in the name of Jesus Christ for the remission of sins, and ye shall receive the gift of the Holy Ghost"*. He spoke of the keys needed to make it into Heaven! These are: 1) repentance, 2) baptism in Jesus' name and 3) the gift of the Holy Ghost.

The Holy Ghost experience is the key. Think perhaps about keys to a new car. One has to have keys to enter into that beautiful new car, but the car will always need **fuel** until the day it dies.

After the Acts 2:38 experience, there has to be daily fuel. I learned this in my early days because I almost ran on empty at times. How many times did the ten virgins fill their lamps with oil? The five virgins with the oil obviously took great care to keep their lamps full and the five without the oil paid a terrible price forever.

Of course, Jesus gave this parable as a sign of the end of time. The oil is the fuel that kept the lamps lit and the Holy Ghost in itself is the initial experience of the lamp's being lit. It must be kept lit with daily fuel of anointed, fiery prayer, which will save us in that great day. It is eternal Heaven or eternal Hell depending on the level of fuel in our lamps and the lives we live! I will say again there is such excitement in the anointing. It is good for this life and for eternal life!

Chapter 2
Drill, Drill, Drill

In 1968, I returned from my military service in Okinawa. During that winter, I went to Vail, Colorado with the title "ski bum." During the first day of skiing, I met the Sam Gary family and skied with them. Sam, who was a great guy, insisted I stay in their condominium. So, I spent the winter with the Gary family. They came from Denver to Vail every weekend. Great folks!

Fast forward to 1976—I had received the Holy Ghost and moved back to Denver. I used my skills to make a living teaching tennis. I let Sam know I taught tennis and within a week he had his pilot fly me to Montana to teach the whole family tennis. Teaching was a gift I had for both skiing and tennis. We had a great week on a beautiful estate on Flathead Lake—it was fun!

After a week, his pilot flew me back to Denver and asked me if I knew Sam's story. I replied that I did not. He proceeded to tell me an amazing story about Sam's 1967 oil drilling experience in Montana. Apparently, Sam had an approximate $100,000 and spent $10,000 for each well. After <u>nine dry wells</u> with enough money for one more shot, he drilled unconventionally at an angle into a hillside. Risky situation!

The last shot produced what became a billion dollar oil field. I had goose bumps. Wow, I thought, he never quit!

So powerful was that story that I have used it in prayer over the years. **Drill, drill, drill** until you hit that well of great anointing which is much more powerful than any billion dollar oil field. I promise!

Chapter 3
One More Cast

I have always enjoyed fishing, and I can promise you that if you want a particular fish, it will demand patience. Case in point: when I was very young, my mom and dad sent me to the St. John's River in Canada with some friends to catch a salmon so they could have a party with fresh salmon.

We were on the river three days and had caught at least a hundred and fifty fish, but not anything over a pound. Frustrated and tired, I wanted to go home. I was not very patient at this point, but we did have one more morning to fish.

We were fly-fishing and my guide was telling me what to do and where to cast. I wanted to leave badly. Little hope remained for a large fish that I did not think existed. I was almost half asleep, when— BANG! The line started singing as this fish took off downstream, leaping into the air as it went. I was shaking with excitement as the guide said, "Wind in or let the fish run." After twenty minutes, he put the net around a fifteen-pound salmon. I stood shaking in disbelief! Needless to say, my mom and dad had their fish and partied.

This thought about the fish has often come to me in prayer. I have prayed and prayed with very little anointing when, after some time—BANG!—the anointing hits with a force as that fish did. It is beyond exciting. How many times could I have quit and walked out of prayer without catching the anointing? Patience in prayer has given me endless victories. I promise it is easy to quit, but the anointing will come!

Chapter 4
Checking the Fuel Gauge

Back in the 1980s, I was driving back to Denver with my business partner, Adolph Coors—and, no, we were not in the Coors Brewery business. As we neared Denver, coming from Omaha, Nebraska, Ad (as we called him) said, "I think we can make it" referring to the gas tank's being on empty. I was nervous as I pictured us walking on the highway having a car with no fuel on the side of the road!

Yes, we did run out of gas, and yes, we did start walking down the highway to get help. No mobile phones existed in the 1980s—it was embarrassing.

I was thankful it was a car out of gas and not a boat way out in the ocean or an airplane about to land short of a runway!

In prayer, the thought of fueling the soul filled me with great revelation! Before I received the Holy Ghost, my "feel good" for the body and soul was alcohol—just one more drink to reach that place of feeling good. The pleasures of sin give a short-lasting temporary high only to drop one hard to the ground the next day.

After I got the Holy Ghost, I switched bottles! I went from bottles of alcohol over to the new Holy Ghost wine and, wow, was that ever exciting!

The thought that came in anointed prayer over the years was "Check your fuel gauge for the soul. Is anger or unforgiveness or any number of issues hindering your anointing?" As time progressed, I needed more anointed fuel to make sure I would make the only flight that will ever matter. I did not want a "stall and stop" experience with my God. I try to keep the tank of anointing (the soul) full, for in that great day of the Lord, the only thing that means anything is the soul going to Heaven! Daily, I check my gauges. We can know if the anointing is flowing!

We have got to make that final flight to be with Jesus for eternity! This Holy Ghost anointing stands alone as the most important daily journey in my life.

Chapter 5
Catch the Wind

In my teenage years, I went to the summer camps of my relatives in the Adirondack Mountains, the home of many lakes. We enjoyed sailing—I clearly remember some of our various sailing adventures. I remember jumping on the sailboat as we pushed away from dock. Some days the winds were really gusting and some days they were not so exciting.

We called the type of wind on mountain lakes "squalls," which is a sharp increase of wind that comes seemingly from out of nowhere.

There was nothing worse than hitting calm areas on the lake. We went to catch some good wind, but at times, just sat in a calm spot in the middle of the lake (which we hated). The sail would flap around and the experience would become boring.

Sometimes I was tempted to jump off the boat and swim to shore. However, invariably, we would look down the lake and see white caps on the water as a squall was building up and heading for our boat! YES!! The wind would abruptly hit the sail and, wow, off we went with the sail over, almost hitting the water. Now that was fun and the calm periods were not! Let me say again that after an extended period of no wind there was a temptation to leave that sorry sailboat in the middle of the lake and swim to shore! But we knew the squalls would return with a vengeance and that was exciting!

The greatest treasure, I promise you, will be a soul on fire for the Lord! As in sailing, so it is with anointed, fiery prayer. So many times in prayer, I hit a calm (no anointing) and in the past I would get up and leave, wondering where the anointed fire and wind of the Holy Ghost was. I basically jumped off the boat!

I learned that Holy Ghost squalls would come in time. Sometimes the "squall" was there waiting to cover me with a great anointing. The Holy Ghost is a spirit and we cannot force it, but we can strive to be in it. Just think, when you are walking in the Spirit, as in the parable of the ten virgins, there will be enough oil to make it to Heaven on that great day of the Lord! I learned to wait in prayer, knowing the winds of the Holy Ghost would blow in time and I promise, it is worth waiting for!

Chapter 6
Give Me the Fire

Many years ago, I watched friends light a match in one hand, dampen the fingers on the other hand and quickly extinguish it. No pain! I did not have enough moisture on my fingers to put the match out, so I felt the burn!

Fire, as we all know, is very dangerous. People who fall asleep with a lit cigarette have caused many fires in which that person and the house are gone—end of life and end of house.

Fire usually starts with a spark or a match in a dry forest and very quickly it is out of control. Endless damage is the result.

Most of all, fires eventually can be put out. Light a match and it is easy—blow it out, but drop the match onto something flammable and it needs to be doused with water very quickly. So many fires can be controlled (such as in a fireplace) and put out if need be, or, left to safely burn out.

I remember the great oil and gas well fires that were started in the Kuwait oil fields in 1991 by the Iraqi military during the Persian Gulf War. Most of these fires were started in January of 1991 and not extinguished until later in the year. I will not go into the technology used to put these fires out, but it was intense—these fires originated from a well in the ground and were exceedingly hot! Deadly!

I have had many prayer meetings where the match of the anointing got lit, but went out in a hurry due to so much going on in my mind.

Over the years, I took control over that problem by digging a deeper well. I have said, "Satan, get out of here in Jesus' name!" The mind is a battleground as everyone knows, but Satan cannot stop you. He can throw the proverbial kitchen sink at you mentally, but I found it was up to me to stay, make sure my life was above reproach, and go for the Holy Ghost fire. Satan cannot put that fire out.

In the past, I let myself be overcome in prayer with the cares of life and just got up and moved on for the day. Not much fire there, but I wanted to live in the fire because I discovered it was exciting when I did get there. John the Baptist mentioned that Jesus would baptize with the Holy Ghost and fire! (Matthew 3:11 "*I indeed baptize you with water unto repentance: but he that cometh after me is mightier than I, whose shoes I am not worthy to bear: he shall baptize you with the Holy Ghost, and with fire:*"

I strive to live in a Holy Ghost oil fire that is hard to be put out and that only I can extinguish by not praying. Once I tasted of this in 1988, I knew I had the answer of fiery anointing and, by the grace of God, I won't let it go. So exciting!

Chapter 7
Hurry Up and Wait

Wow! I've been in the waiting rooms of many births—my children, grandchildren, and children of friends. The excitement is always high. I remember thinking, "Will the baby be healthy, will it have hair, how heavy will it be, etc.," but at certain times, I got tired of waiting. No one can do anything but wait; or wait and wait; or wait, wait, and wait. The baby is coming at some point, but patience is essential.

The worst case scenarios can be, "Get to the hospital fast!" One rushes to the hospital only to find out the mother was in false or premature labor. No baby, no excitement! Starting the waiting process all over is tiring, but the baby will be born!

I remember the harsh winter of January at Fort Dix during basic training many years ago, while I was in the military. The common words I especially remember were, "Hurry up and wait!" I really hated that because many of us were sweating outside in bitter cold weather after a work out. We had to wait outside and freeze before getting changed. There was a lot of sickness and yes, I got very sick. So many times we got where we were supposed to be in a great hurry and then had to wait!

I do not think waiting is anyone's favorite pastime. Red lights, traffic jams, and doctor's offices are just a few places that we have to endure.

But there is one place I have learned to wait, and wait I will, because I know what is on the way! Prayer can be tenuous to many. For years, I spent a little time in prayer and that was it. But waiting on the Lord is one of the most blessed things I have learned. I know if I wait long enough in prayer, that great blessing of anointing is going to come!

I can honestly say that hurry up and wait in the military was horrible, but "hurry up, get to church and wait on the Lord" has many, many joyous benefits!

Chapter 8
Greatest Health and Healing Product There Is!

Well, if anyone would ask me, I would say I believe in health and fitness. I have for many years, but have not always lived up to my commitments. I went through a devastating ten-year period of anxiety, fear, and depression while in the church. I remember going to health store after health store trying products for depression and anxiety. I wasted hundreds of dollars with absolutely no results.

There had to be answers or I was ready to die and leave this world. Yes, I was praying—for years—without feeling much, but in my very darkest hours, I knew the Lord was the same and did not change. Many times I just prayed to let the Lord know I still loved Him. Deep, deep in prayer in Vermont, the Lord laid on my heart to forgive some people. That was one of the very greatest prayers of my life!! I had always attempted to forgive from the mind and I promise that did not work. I did not understand forgiveness from the heart, but talk about healing and health coming back—and anointing!! What else can I say?

Recently, I felt such a revelation in prayer that anointed, fiery prayer was the greatest health and healing product in the world that I texted my thought to Bishop Holmes. In less than a minute, he texted back in capital letters, "AMEN!"

17

So many times I have had answers to health issues just happen in prayer. III John 2 *"Beloved, I wish above all things that thou mayest prosper and be in health, even as thy SOUL PROSPERETH."* The soul will prosper greatly with anointed prayer, but what else does it say—prosperity and health. Great, great Scripture!

I had severe chest pains recently that lasted for two years. I followed up with a great cardiologist who gave me excellent results on an echo stress test. That was a target test. ALL GLORY TO GOD!

Yes, by revelation, I declare fiery, anointed prayer to be the greatest health and healing product on the planet. Bishop Holmes gave me an "AMEN" to that revelation. What can I do but glorify the Lord?

Some of the facts of what the medical world says need to go on the back burner so you can take that faith to a new level!

Chapter 9
U.S. Air Force vs Chinese Air Force

Many years ago when I was drafted into the Army, they put me into Military Intelligence. I am not sure how that happened, but so be it. I spent three months in Maryland training for Military Intelligence and then was sent off to Okinawa for a year and a half. At that time, the Vietnam War was at its peak—1966 and 1967.

Our job was to keep track of all the people who used aliases or AKAs (Also Known As) in Okinawa. We had names of folks that had up to twenty-five or more identities. They all were Okinawans that showed displeasure with America and our military. Some were in jail; some were not.

We had many jobs—one was to keep large wall maps of the war zones in Vietnam. We got intelligence in daily briefings as to where the troops were located on both sides of the war. We had many U.S. and Viet Cong positions to locate daily. I had some fun doing this job. I could have easily been in the rice paddies in the war trying to duck bullets, so over all, my service time was not a bad situation.

As time progressed, my service time was slowly coming to an end and I was very happy about that. But the last few days on The Rock, as we called it, I learned of one event that happened every day, which was a little scary to me. The air space around Okinawa was challenged everyday by Chinese jet fighters and the U.S. Air Force challenged back. There were never any incidents, but it brought to mind that the war between good and evil is tested everyday—not only in the air space between Okinawa and China, but in all things. Every day, challenges between good and evil exist. Millions of Americans are caught up in alcohol and the alarming effect of drugs. The effect of television is now loaded with pure evil. Parents are fighting to make the right decisions for their children with the morbid immorality on college campuses.

Then it all came together in prayer. Satan will test our Holy Ghost space as the Chinese did in Okinawa! And I say again, he will test it and the Lord will allow him to do so. If I miss a day of prayer due to sickness, I will feel it!

Good is fighting evil and evil is fighting good. And yes, the day has arrived where many call evil "good" and good "evil."

I discovered I can be almost immune to all the evil thoughts and events with daily, fiery, anointed prayer. It is totally amazing what takes place in the spiritual realm with the Lord. Where evil wanted to prevail, goodness of the Lord prevailed!

I literally was going to make decisions that would have been horrible, but after walking with the Lord in the anointing, good came out of a bad situation.

It is an absolute that fiery, anointed prayer will fight evil and save our souls! I know of nothing else that will work.

Chapter 10
Casting All Your Care Upon Him

The Scripture took me many years to get ahold of! 1 Peter 5:7 *"Casting all your care (*anxiety*) upon him; for he careth for you."* How many, many times over the years did I go to the church and pray, casting my cares upon the Lord, to then get up from prayer, walk out the door and guess what? All those cares and anxieties were still with me! I knew the Lord's words through Paul were true, but what was my problem?

I got my real answer to that Scripture many years later, but it did not have to be many years later. Was it my fault? I believe the Scripture was totally true, but as Bishop Holmes would ask, "Were you plugged in?" (He was referring to the powerful anointing of the Lord).

In my formative years in Christ, many different Bible Scriptures had a learning curve and 1 Peter 5:7 was definitely one of them. Over the years, I developed a relationship with the Lord and slowly began to understand the meaning of that Scripture. Here is my simple secret to all of this!

If a person has a true relationship with a friend, their children, their husband or wife, and the Lord, things begin to happen, I promise. As the anointing in fiery, anointed prayer grew in my life, so many of the real cares of this life began to evaporate! If we do not have a relationship with the Lord, He may not be fully listening. He will give us divine attention if we are deep in intercessory prayer. Speaking in tongues in the Holy Ghost is the ultimate!

Case in point (and I could give many): a few weeks ago, I was in prayer when I got a text message from my realtor regarding the house we have been trying to sell for a year. I knew there was an appointment for a showing and, one hour into prayer, I received a text from the realtor who was showing the house. It was a temporary slug to my soul. The text from the client who viewed the house to my realtor was, "The house needs work and updating." Ouch!

I believe because I have attempted to be faithful in prayer, the Lord lifted my spirit and away from that text in a moment. I felt great power for the next forty-five minutes! Then, guess what? My realtor was amazed—we had an offer and the house sold to that buyer! Thank you, Jesus!

In the past, I would have walked out of the church and became downtrodden. The devil would have laughed. It was my choice to dig a little deeper and, with the Lord's divine intervention, we climbed higher. What a blessing that was! Deeper, higher— roots deeper, branches higher and with more fruit!

A daily feast of anointed, fiery prayer will keep many cares (anxieties) from tangling my mind into knots. So many troubling issues will just melt away with daily prayer. Do they attempt to return throughout the day and the night? Yes, but usually with minimal effects.

A few chapters back, I mentioned the American Air Force and the Chinese Air Force challenging each other daily. Good versus evil! So many, many doors are unlocked with prayer and one of the main ones is when I pray in the anointing, the cares that I cast before the Lord are minimized or destroyed. I am aware there can be a time element, but our dear friend "patience" will certainly help! Patience, I know, is not our favorite, but it has glowing, delicious fruit in time!

Chapter 11
Where is God?

In my forty-six years of serving the Lord, I have had many moments of wondering where the Lord is. I often felt that when I called on Him there was a busy signal, He didn't answer His phone or He was out for the day and did not want to hear me.

I learned over time that God is not an icemaker, a car, a radio, or anything else that allows you to punch a button or turn on a key to get instant results. We live in a day of instant gratification! I want it now and I mean right now, whatever it might be. We are Americans! I love America, but to touch the heart of the Lord takes time and a relationship with Him. Perhaps many just want the fishes and loaves. Wal-mart and many malls are filled with stuff. People want stuff and they want it now!

I told my wife that I always felt I would get mauled at the mall. I have seen couples at stores where he says, "No." She says, "We have to have it" (whatever it is) and he says, "No, we don't need it." I move on before the fireworks start. We have so much, but I learned years ago that a vital part of my life was missing. I asked the Lord in 1988 for an intercessory prayer life; He heard me and hundreds of hours of anointed, fiery prayer has followed!

One of the greatest times in life was eating from my mother's table. She had a big garden every year. It was harvested in the summer and we had lots of fresh peas, corn, strawberries, lima beans, and on and on. She froze a lot as well, so we always had great food. The process, of course, took many hours, but the reward was great—fresh, healthy food. Today, food that is processed with preservatives is dangerous. One famous person said in this day that if you get your food through a fast food window, it is probably not very good for you. The process of building a relationship with the Lord, like Mom's garden, takes a little more time.

I have often wondered what might cause a disconnect from the Lord. At times in my life, there were things in my heart that would block the real presence of the Lord. A huge spiritual block was *lack of forgiveness*. I could not get through in prayer because I had been wronged. When forgiveness takes place as it did in my case after ten years, Heaven opens up again!

So many times people ask, "Where is God?" Some have cried out, but no response, no answers, nothing. Jesus Christ wants a deep relationship with all that have the Holy Ghost. I got the Holy Ghost in 1971, but I did not develop a fiery, intercessory prayer life until 1988. I prayed for two months to receive the Holy Ghost and over the years I kept a little oil in the lamp, but the Lord wanted more. Was I one of the ten virgins in the parable that hardly had enough oil to make this final journey? Only He would know. Mercy and grace are needed greatly by all, but I have to do my part. Great joy and power came with this prayer.

As my well of anointing has gotten deeper and deeper, it has not been hard to find the Lord on a daily basis. Answers to situations often come before I really ask Him. Walking very close to the Lord just brings answers!

So where is God? He is down deep in the well of anointing and I will say that many of my prayers are now answered because of my very deep relationship with the Lord! Oh yes, lest I forget, many times I have learned there is a waiting time. That is what it takes for there to be oil in my lamp in case of the Lord's coming! Again, I say, by the mercy and grace of the Lord. The first part of James 4:8 instructs us to *"Draw nigh to God and He will draw nigh to you."* I promise you that if you will go deep into the well, it is heart to heart with the Lord and very exciting!

Chapter 12
The Real Wrestling Match

Ephesians 6:12 tells us *"For we wrestle not against flesh and blood, but against principalities, against powers, against the rulers of the darkness of this world, against spiritual wickedness in high places."* In the past, I rarely viewed wrestling matches, but the few times I did, I noticed the individuals that were involved were grunting and gasping for air. It is a very intense ordeal in which one person works feverishly to pin their opponent to the floor. If the judge or referee counts to ten while the loser has his shoulders pinned to the floor, a winner is declared.

I will be honest in saying I never had any desire to be a wrestler. I just liked other sports. But in 1988, when I asked the Lord to bring intercessory prayer into my life, that prayer began a day later at one in the morning! I started to recall the scripture I quoted at the beginning of this chapter and began tying my actions of groaning and interceding and speaking in tongues to wrestling in the Spirit. I was not wrestling against flesh and blood. I knew very well what was going on in the spiritual realm.

That type of prayer has been extremely intense through the Holy Ghost over many years. I have cried, screamed, and groaned nightly in the Holy Ghost! Spirits have been destroyed or have retreated. Many doors in my life that were rusted shut just fell down. Outreach in my life when to supernatural levels. In 1988-1992, doors were opened to witness on nationwide shows, to professional athletes, and to many other groups in Jesus' name!

If you look at the rulers of darkness in this world, they sit in high places as dictators and kings. That is where Satan can really pervert issues, such as our own Supreme Court passing gay marriage as the law of the land. The Lord hates that life style (*see scripture references below), but that law came from the Supreme Court, so here we are. In time, the Supreme Court will lose out to the Supreme King, Jesus Christ!

In fiery, anointed prayer, I can feel the Lord pushing back on all spirits! Remember Sodom and Gomorrah, they did not fare very well with that lifestyle and in time, we will not either. Do I ever feel like wrestling against flesh and blood? Yes! Will I? With the help of the Lord, no, I will not, but day and night I fight against many spirits for the sake of all. It is wrestling in the Holy Ghost prayer that will win out now and in the end, I promise. We must keep our lamps filled with the oil! The rulers of the darkness of the world are, in many cases, wicked. They take money from the people, kill Christians, are mostly billionaires, and may be demon-possessed.

Spiritual wickedness in high places is this: when a leader in a high spiritual place declares something is good that the Lord hates, the people under these rulers often accept that which is immoral and wrong. I have thought about how perverse our generation is all over the world. It is terrible, but the fantastic news is that day and night, I get to the wrestling mat in the house of the Lord and win out with peace. That also helps me to be kind to all people. Isaiah 26:3, *"Thou wilt keep him in perfect peace, whose mind is stayed on thee: because he trusteth in thee."* How does that happen? Prayer, prayer, prayer will bring answers that come from the supernatural, I promise!

How many times in our great country do I daily hear the lies of the media, political leaders, and some college professors? Always; but I get to the house of the Lord in fiery, anointed prayer and come out the victor in Jesus' name!

Bishop Holmes, our great man of God, has said numerous times over the years, "I have a hard enough time changing myself and I sure cannot change others." I have thought about this many times and it is true.

I have wanted at various times in my life to change some things and through prayer and effort, my great God has helped me make some changes! It works!

*Leviticus 18:22 *"Thou shalt not lie with mankind, as with womankind: it is abomination."*

*Leviticus 20:13 *"If a man also lie with mankind, as he lieth with a woman, both of them have committed an abomination: they shall surely be put to death; their blood shall be upon them."*

*Romans 1:26, 27 *"For this cause God gave them up into vile affections: for even their women did change the natural use into that which is against nature. And likewise also the men, leaving the natural use of the woman, burned in their lust one toward another; men with men working that which is unseemly, and receiving in themselves that recompence of their error which was meet."*

*I Corinthians 6:9 *"Know ye not that the unrighteous shall not inherit the kingdom of God? Be not deceived: neither fornicators, nor idolaters, nor adulterers, nor effeminate, nor abusers of themselves with mankind,"*

Chapter 13
The Opiate of Anointing

An opiate is a product derived from opium to reduce pain. It is wrongly abused many times for fighting emotional pain and physical pain. There is an epidemic of opiate misuse in America that is killing vast numbers of people.

In 1843, Karl Marx said religion is the opiate of the people. Many people in the day of Karl Marx conjured for themselves sources of phony happiness to help numb the pain of reality. And where are we today in the world? Numbing the pain of a broken marriage, a lost job, or the death of a friend are some of the issues people use opiates for to pivot from what their perceived reality is. Most issues people tangle with deal with how to escape the reality of the here and now.

Forty-six years ago, before receiving the Holy Ghost, my escape route from daily tasks of life was alcohol. Alcohol almost took me off the cliff into eternity. Certainly, I was very lost and going the wrong way—in fact, right into a mental institution!

Growing up, I was always troubled by the questions, "What is reality, who am I, where am I going, and when will I die?" I used sports, along with other events, to wrap myself up with stuff so I did not have to do a lot of "here and now" thinking.

So what is reality? As I studied this subject, I found it too vast to give a simple answer from the world's point of view. Folks will travel everywhere to find a new opiate of religion—whether it is sports, politics or something else. The Bible is the only reality I know.

Some folks are living to get an education and wind up becoming professional students. They are still in school at fifty years of age; still trying to find out who they are.

Many people live in denial of the issues of life. In my past, there were any number of situations that I was in denial of. For me, drinking was a great pastime to temporarily blot out angers. Of course, it created more angers!

In 1971, at the very end of my rope of life, I searched and prayed the best I could for reality. Was it God or something else? I wanted my head to work again; I had a broken brain, which is worse than a broken bone. I was drowning in fear, anxiety, and depression. My heart, mind, and soul were on a search for the real reality. Thank God, I found it on June 1st, 1971 at two in the morning!

I received, through the grace of God, my feel good, my opiate—the Holy Ghost! In my early life, I had created so many false realities that a few friends thought I had gone completely crazy! Speaking in tongues as the Spirit gave utterance was absolute peace with no hangover!

Over forty-six years, especially the last thirty years, I have developed my opiate of anointing, found complete reality, and am so excited that I pass out written testimonies on a daily basis. I promise you, it is a "feel good" experience as Bishop Holmes calls it!

Everything I tried to hold to as my foundation of life crumbled. I did look into and study a lot of belief systems only to be engulfed by emptiness. If you feel I am boasting about my prayer life, I am—in the Lord. The answer is getting something for your soul and then daily manna from Heaven to fill it, which is fiery, anointed prayer. Forty-six years now of a real life in Christ, Holy Ghost, and the many hours of prayer that nurture it, have been the answer!

The opiate of the anointing is a very "feel good" experience and I want it every day. Praying in the Spirit is very hard to describe, but in many cases it minimizes the pain of this world! I taught our children to walk a vertical life, looking upward to see the Lord. Walking a horizontal experience is devastating. Watching others, hearing the news and events of the day can be depressing. The vertical walk in the Spirit of much anointed prayer is truly an opiate to the perilous times we live in!

Chapter 14
Walking in the Spirit

August 2, 2006 was my personal Pearl Harbor day. I had been dealing with kidney stones since mid-July of that year. I made six trips to the emergency room for pain medications. "Drink more water and take your medications," were the instructions for the first three trips. The fourth trip was a non-invasive surgery called lithotripsy. This is a procedure in which shock waves are used to break up the stones without any invasion of the body. It can be very successful. This time though, the lithotripsy did not work.

The very next day was my fifth trip to the emergency room and it was probably the most troublesome. I was experiencing a lot of kidney pain and fever, so the doctor felt one more round of lithotripsy would take care of the kidney stone. My wife, Linda, and son-in-law, Wade Townley, went with me. Once again, I was heavily sedated for an extended period of time. In fact, I felt pain in my semi-conscious state so they added more sedation medications.

At the end of the procedure, my wife and Wade were in the waiting room. Linda had a sandwich and iced drink for me. I felt pretty good, obviously from the medications. We left the hospital and in a few minutes arrived at JoAnn's (Linda's mom's) apartment. Within seconds of arriving, I knew something had gone terribly wrong. I had a pain level I had never known. I was literally going insane with pain.

Linda called Wade and took me back to the ER. I was on the floor and out of my mind. From what I can remember, I was loaded with morphine and by two the next morning, I was in a semi-comatose state in the hospital. I was gasping for air. It was a surreal state. I was told later that an x-ray showed nothing. Some doctor thought I was just having an anxiety attack. Apparently, another doctor ordered a CAT scan right away that showed numerous blood clots in my lungs.

And so, the life and death journey began—forty days and nights in the belly of the hospital. I am going to throw in a "Thank You, Jesus!" in the middle of this—Thank You, JESUS!!

The daily battle started the next morning between the doctors! We discovered what had happened—the lithotripsy had caused a peripheral hematoma. In English, a kidney had been cut by the shock waves.

Thank God I lived through the first round of the pulmonary embolisms! I was now on oxygen. The medical battle between two doctors was underway. One was saying that, "He has to have blood thinners because the next clot could kill him." The other was saying, "Blood thinners will cause the kidney to bleed again from the cut and that could kill him!" I say again, "THANK YOU, JESUS"!

I had no fear. The morphine was in use and the Lord was kind. The fuse was lit—which way would I go? I had a filter inserted to stop clots from going to my lungs.

It was two weeks into this disaster when my legs began to hurt, swell, and develop blood clots overnight. I kept punching the nurse call button asking if there was a doctor on call. There was not.

All I can remember of the next morning is doctors and nurses surrounding my bed. Apparently, my left leg was without any feeling and turning color. My right leg was also dying and losing feeling. This was the end of anything I could remember.

My daughter, Kara, walked into Saturday morning prayer when my other daughter, Sharon, called from the hospital to say all of my vital signs were shutting down. Kara was crying! Bishop Holmes entered the church and Kara told him the bad news. Bishop Holmes began to smile and told her that her dad was going to be all right. He then proceeded to call my wife Linda to say that I was not going to lose a kidney or a leg.

It took me a few months to even realize what our man of God, who daily walks in the Spirit, had said. I had to put this miracle together in my mind over time. How could Bishop Holmes smile at Kara and say to her, "He is going to be all right," when the ones at the hospital were about to look for a body bag?

If a man of God truly walks in the Spirit, these miracles happen and continue to happen! Thank You, Jesus for a praying man of God!

Chapter 15
What Dominates the Soul?

Years ago, I heard a story of a lady who was invited to a Denver Bronco's football game. She hated football and just about everything else. Her boyfriend insisted that she should go to just one game and she hesitantly, and disdainfully agreed. Apparently, this woman started cheering with everyone else as the action of the play began to excite her. I heard that she got with it in a big way and all of a sudden this person was a fan. As I heard the story, the Denver Broncos became her god. She lived and died for the next game and of course, over time, could not wait for the next Bronco season. She finally had something to dominate her soul!

As I thought about this chapter, it became clear to me that whatever interest or addiction dominates one's soul becomes their god. In a sense, this woman served the Broncos. She gave them her money.

From a young age, my god, my life, my all, was sports. I lived and died, or almost died, for the god of my sports life. If our team lost, I would use many inappropriate words. When I started playing tennis years ago, the tennis rackets were made out of wood. When I lost, I had a tendency to break rackets by smashing them on the court. I was a sore, sore loser.

That, in time, led to excessive anger in my life. I did not like losing, so I found something else to serve and pay for and that was alcohol. I remember drinking my first beer. It tasted awful! But it had a little buzz to it so it added a little joy to my soul. In time, I went full-bore on alcohol. It satisfied my soul, might I say, for just moments! Headaches and anger followed and I said, "I will never do this again" (get drunk that is). But that god of alcohol had complete dominion over my soul. It was a "feel good" experience. Sin has a pleasure for a season! And the next night, I was drunk again.

I remember my study of scientology, Christian Science, and other things that gave me hope for my soul. The soul of man is always on a search for peace, joy, and happiness. I promise, wealth will not satisfy a soul. Been there, done that!

Everyone, whether they admit it or not, searches for real peace, joy, and happiness. In my youth, I did not know where it could be found. After the pure horror and vision of Hell I experienced in 1970 while institutionalized, I had to have answers or die.

I visited my sister in Denver, was invited to a Pentecostal church, and received the baptism of the Holy Ghost. I was not out of the tunnel, but for the first time in my life, I could see the light at the end of a very long, dark tunnel!

As I have told many people, I just switched

bottles to the new wine! Read Acts 2:13-17 *"Others mocking said, These men are full of new wine. But Peter, standing up with the eleven, lifted up his voice, and said unto them, Ye men of Judaea, and all ye that dwell at Jerusalem, be this known unto you, and hearken to my words: For these are not drunken, as ye suppose, seeing it is but the third hour of the day. But this is that which was spoken by the prophet Joel; And it shall come to pass in the last days, saith God, I will pour out of my Spirit upon all flesh: and your sons and your daughters shall prophesy, and your young men shall see visions, and your old men shall dream dreams."* Basically, when the Holy Ghost was poured out, the folks in the crowd thought the apostles and others who received the Holy Ghost were drunk with the wrong stuff, but it was the Holy Ghost!

For forty-six years, cultures have changed over and over, dress styles have changed, hairstyles have changed, but my experience for my soul and my lifestyle has not changed! Living in daily, fiery, anointed prayer will keep a soul contented. The Lord is happy for He created the soul of man to inhabit it. I am happy and after forty-six years, I want to become a greater Holy Ghostaholic!

Chapter 16
Plaque

In America today, most all people have some level of that gooey yellow substance in our blood vessels called plaque. When this substance builds up enough and the flow of blood is impeded, we have chest pain. When the vessel walls have even more build up over time, we have a heart attack. Where does plaque originate? It comes from eating too many processed foods with excessive preservatives, fatty meats, too much sugar, and so forth. I have studied health for years and learned a good deal about food. I will also add that stress over time does not help plaque levels either.

Our bodies are the temple of the Holy Ghost. I have, in the past, totally abused this temple. Before Christ (B.C.) I was fueled with alcohol and any junk food I wanted to eat. After I received the Holy Ghost, the alcohol was gone, but junk food was easily available. I would grab a donut, and another donut, and a coke, and more and more junk food. In my youth, I could get away with this and now, thank the Lord, I cannot! Blood numbers do not lie! We do lie though and I did lie about what I ate. The truth will always be in the blood numbers. Yes, for a while, I thought I could trick the blood tests, but it will not happen. I would have a bad insulin number and the doctor said that I needed to cut the sweets. Then I got an elevated uric acid number and was told I needed to cut back on proteins. My very nature is stubborn towards what I eat, but death will knock at my door if I do not pay attention to the blood analysis. Many folks do not pay attention and opt out for a drug. Many of those drugs will mess up their health a little more. I know this personally.

If this temple of the Holy Ghost, our body, is destroyed with the wrong foods, it puts a weight on our prayer life. I have been there and done that! So we all know bad choices in eating habits can destroy and kill the temple (the body) of the Holy Ghost. One last comment on this physical body: many are dying from diabetes which leads to cancer and heart disease and a host of other diseases. So when I saw some bad numbers in my blood, I went to work on them and yes, by the grace of God, I reversed them!

Moving to an extremely important thought: what about spiritual plaque that could end our hopes of making it to Heaven? When I received the Holy Ghost, my life changed radically, thank the Lord. What I read, what I listened to, what I drank, and my fledgling tennis career of organized sports all came to an abrupt end. It was not a man who changed this; it was the Lord, through the convictions I gained upon receiving the Holy Ghost, and I thank God for that! The thought of spiritual plaque has always gotten my attention. The night a person receives the Holy Ghost is a cleaning up of all their fleshly gods. These are replaced with the truth and spirit of Jesus Christ. The Holy Ghost had the power to deliver me from many fleshly desires. I had a very clean spiritual vessel, as everyone does, after that great experience. It cleaned out my soul of all the issues that almost destroyed my life.

Was I delivered immediately from the fear, anxiety, and depression that possessed my life? No! But the victory was in sight!! Sadly, many I have known have allowed this to be a one-time experience and the ways of the world, without the daily, anointed prayer, took control of their lives again.

If you weed a garden, it looks great! But if the weeds are not controlled, the good fruit of the garden will be destroyed; so it is with our soul. In life, evil thoughts and temptations of the past will beat on the door of my soul. This is the reality of a walk with God. I used to think that bad thoughts would destroy my life. That is exactly what the devil wanted me to think. In my early walk with the Lord, I learned that prayer (and I did not have a great prayer life) would ward off that which was evil. In time, as the fire of prayer was developed, I was able, through the anointing, to fight the fire of evil! I John 4:4 *"...because greater is he that is in you, than he that is in the world."*

Dying out daily, as the Apostle Paul did, is essential to salvation. I remember years ago, when living in Denver, I would listen to a few minutes of a football game or some music of the 1960s. I was convicted by the Holy Ghost to turn away from all the things I once loved. In time, having a fiery, anointed prayer life pretty much turned me away from my past.

The Holy Ghost, coupled with mercy and grace, will certainly prepare us for our final journey for eternity. I absolutely believe in Heaven and Hell and, with the complete help of the Lord, the journey to Heaven with a clean spiritual vessel is very possible. It is so easy for the plaque of the world to plug up our spiritual vessels. Just as the flesh will die from plugged blood vessels, so will the spiritual man perish from the sin of this world.

Chapter 17
Fervent Prayer

Fervent prayer is hot, burning, glowing, intense, passionate, and vehement prayer. The second part of James 5:16 speaks of this: *"The effectual fervent prayer of a righteous man availeth much."*

Many years ago when I prayed, occasionally someone would say that God could hear me—I did not need to be loud and fervent in my prayer. I would say God bless these folks, but I was born in the fire and I am going to stay in the fire. I am very amused at how much fervency the world has for their gods. I remember many years ago attending some pro-sports events—professional hockey, baseball and football to name a few. I can promise you that being quiet is not part of the sports world. There was incessant screaming, hollering, and worshiping of the sports gods.

A few years ago, I spoke with a friend of mine who had attended a basketball game the night before. When we spoke, he almost had no voice. The game, to him, was so exciting he screamed until he was hoarse! They serve their gods by paying to see them and then screaming and shouting for them. Did I scream at athletic events before I switched from the gods of concerts and sports to the God of righteousness, Jesus Christ? Yes, I screamed with great fervency. I got into it big time. But forty-six years ago I switched from the many gods of this world to one God! And for all these years, I have screamed, hollered, shouted, and worshipped Jesus Christ with great fervency. My God does not have me down and out with a hangover. It is unbelievable what the Lord does. I will cry out to the Lord without even feeling His presence because I know Who He is! And, as I have described in previous chapters, He shows up. Maybe right away, maybe ten minutes or even an hour into my prayer, I feel that great fiery anointing or better said, the absolute presence of the Lord. It is supernatural and definitely an overdose of the earnest of our inheritance of Heaven to come.

For many years, I have thought about why I screamed and shouted at concerts or sporting events. What drove that intensity? I mean, my soul was on fire for the next touchdown or home run. What I came up with is that all sports have a worship-like effect on their fans and, yes, I was one of those. In fact, it is a very powerful worship of a sports god or concert god. And I paid those gods!

In 1964, the Beatles showed up in America. What I felt when I heard their first song on the radio is, "Wow, this feels good." As some can remember, their singing just took over America back in the day. In fact, John Lennon, their lead singer, said that they would become greater than Jesus Christ. That was poorly thought out. John was shot and killed as he entered his apartment in New York City in 1980.

Over many years, I decided that I would not let my worship of the gods of this world take a higher priority to my prayer in the Holy Ghost. I have cried out for many years to Jesus Christ more so than to the gods of this world.

The first outpouring of the Holy Ghost in Acts 2:1-4 was not a quiet experience, *"And when the day of Pentecost was fully come, they were all with one accord in one place. And suddenly there came a sound from heaven as of a rushing mighty wind, and it filled all the house where they were sitting. And there appeared unto them cloven tongues like as of fire, and it sat upon each of them. And they were all filled with the Holy Ghost, and began to speak with other tongues, as the Spirit gave them utterance."* And if anyone ever received the Holy Ghost without going into intense physical, spiritual, and emotional worship, I would be shocked.

The soul, when filled with what it was designed to be filled with (the Holy Ghost), should experience a daily, fiery, exciting infilling. The oil in the lamps of the five wise virgins allowed the fire to burn. The other five had no fire—could that be the Holy Ghost?— because there was no fuel (oil) in their lamps and they were not saved.

My desperate, daily prayer life is not for the fishes and loaves, but because of my relationship with the Lord! Read Psalms 22:5 *"They cried unto thee, and were delivered: they trusted in thee, and were not confounded"* and Psalms 107:6 *"Then they cried unto the Lord in their trouble, and he delivered them out of their distresses."*

I close this chapter with one more example of a fervent cry to the Lord. In 1970, when searching for life's answers while institutionalized, I vividly remember speaking to a man in a wheelchair. He all but cursed God, saying basically, there is no God. A few days later, I heard a man screaming over and over, "Please, God, help me!" It was that same fellow in the wheelchair. Perhaps he had a troubling, drug experience. There are no real atheists when trouble comes! They also cry out to the Lord!

Chapter 18
The Last Resort of Hope

Many who seek the experience of the Holy Ghost are desperate for answers or have a hunger for righteousness to overcome a life of problems, whatever they might be. I was hungering for answers to overcome fear, anxiety, and depression. Matthew 5:6 says, *"Blessed are they which do hunger and thirst after righteousness: for they shall be filled."* In 1971, I was starved for answers. I wanted the Lord in my life. I was desperate for help because my life was dwindling away.

Recently, I spoke with Bishop Holmes about the people I wanted to see get the Holy Ghost. His comment back to me was that there is no hope unless they are hungry! I have always known that, but I thought I could help people get hungry. In my early days, I let some people close to me know it was the Holy Ghost or Hell. I promise, there were no results except some very angry people. The Lord has to convict and call people, and I learned our job is to plant and water and let the Lord give the increase.

I have studied I Corinthians 3:6-8 over the years, *"I have planted, Apollos watered; but God gave the increase. So then neither is he that planteth any thing, neither he that watereth; but God that giveth the increase. Now he that planteth and he that watereth are one: and every man shall receive his own reward according to his own labour.*" I have had many different formats of my testimony to give out to people, praying someone would be hungry. Many, many visitors have come and thank the Lord a few have received the Holy Ghost!

I remember churches filled up after 9/11. There was fear in America for what might come next. The stock market had a big drop for a short time. In 1988, someone wrote a book on eighty-eight reasons the Lord would come back in 1988. He made a lot of money. I also heard reports of those who received the Holy Ghost for fear of missing the Lord's return. Of course, we all know that foxholes have no atheists during war! The Lord created our soul for His pleasure to bless us and we, in return, bless Him. It is a great experience.

But I want to delve a little deeper into this subject about why people seek the Holy Ghost. There is a hunger caused by a problem somewhere in their soul, as it was in my case. In forty-six years, I have seen many people come and go. They receive the Holy Ghost and the Lord starts blessing. Good things start happening in their lives and many times, once the contentment sets in, there is a little Holy Ghost fuel to keep that fire burning. Then, due to little or no prayer, the fire goes out and out the door that person goes. Maybe God gave that person a good job, more money, more blessings, saved a marriage, or any number of blessings, but again, I say the only fuel we have to keep the fire of the Holy Ghost alive and burning is anointed, fiery prayer.

I have learned over and over to wait for the anointing in prayer and when it does come, it is so exciting that the time flies!

So to finalize this chapter, God wants a relationship with us. He does not want us to have a "fish and loaves" experience where we beg Him for things, because that is short-lived. Many years ago, a man I knew who was somewhat backslid said to me, "God promised me money." I do not think he survived his walk with the Lord. I will promise that if a person has a great relationship with the Lord through daily, anointed prayer, good things just happen. I do not seek things; I seek Him and guess what? It is amazing. Matthew 6:33 tells us, *"But seek ye first the kingdom of God, and his righteousness; and all these things shall be added unto you."* If we work His plan, I promise, He will work for us! Relationships can have great rewards, but a great relationship with the Lord is supernatural!

Chapter 19
Hidden Sin in Life

In many prayer meetings, I will ask the Lord to search my heart and soul for any areas in which I might have wronged somebody or where someone did wrong to me and I did not forgive that person. I consider searching my heart almost daily to be extremely important as to whether or not the Lord blesses me. We all can bury certain pains in life and eventually they become sins (because many times they are issues of unforgiveness). A seed of bitterness can be repented of quickly, but if it gets a root to it, then there is more work to be done.

Case in point: I remember hearing a story about a lady getting hit from behind by another driver quite some time ago. She had spinal injuries and lost her license because of the injuries she received. It absolutely was not her fault, but she struggled with health problems from that day on. Twenty years later, she met someone who asked her if she had ever forgiven the man that hit the back of her car. She said she had not. They had a lengthy talk and at the end of the visit she wanted to forgive the man, but didn't know where he was. She had a sincere prayer and desire to forgive that man. She never found him, but before the Lord, she was able to forgive him from her heart. She was healed almost immediately! Wow, how powerful forgiveness is in the eyes of the Lord!

Many times, when an offender is approached and you want to forgive him, he just will not acknowledge what he did and can become angry. If the offender gets angry and you forgive them, that is his or her problem. I have forgiven a few folks through prayer to the Lord just as that lady did. God hears us when we are desperate and mean business. Denial is a big problem for many people—I know it was for me. We want to deny what happened when we were deeply hurt. We bury it deep in the subconscious and in time it can come out in heart disease, cancer, or depression, which is what happened to me. Jesus forgave and we have to forgive. It can be a process, but it can and must be done.

Is it sin when we are hurt and in shock? No, but over time, it builds and we bury it deeper and deeper. We become bitter with pain, and then it becomes sin. I have heard comments from people of, "How could he or she do this to me?" I have read many stories of battered wives or abused children who will not acknowledge their abuser out of fear. Eventually, all this pain will come out and only through a very deep relationship with the Lord can forgiveness be obtained. Sadly, many die of bitterness. It is a known fact that hurt people often hurt other people.

It took me ten years of terrible suffering to understand forgiveness, but when I did, the Lord gave me a giant step toward getting my health back!

I have had small things come to me in prayer that the Lord laid on my heart to do and, by the grace of God, I listened. Bishop Holmes calls them "nudges."

I was able to forgive the doctor that cut my kidney the next day while I was in a critical condition. I understood unforgiveness from 2003, which almost killed me with depression. In prayer, our Holy Ghost radar will tap our soul to forgive before it becomes sin. Help me, oh Lord, to be sensitive!

Chapter 20
Can Satan Keep Me Out of Heaven?

The answer to this question, as I have learned over the years, is NO! Bishop Holmes has taught well on this subject. When I got the Holy Ghost at age twenty-four, I honestly thought Satan could stop me from making it to Heaven. I was troubled on and off by that fear.

As I have said, I did not develop an anointed, fiery prayer life until 1988 even though I received the Holy Ghost in 1971. My wife and I had prayer for five to ten minutes every night with Seth, Kara and Sharon. We also arrived at church early on Sundays for prayer and occasionally had a Friday night prayer meeting. The Lord had mercy on us for the little prayer we had in our early years. My prayer tank stayed on empty some of the time, but thank God that we got by.

I have always wanted to improve my life in Christ. Over the years, as I grew stronger in the Lord, I started realizing that no, Satan directly could not keep me out of Heaven. I felt it was a very serious issue and it certainly is. I heard so many stories of "the devil made me do it" or other reasons people got tangled up with the devil. It took time, but I finally realized the devil could do nothing if I stayed out of his traps!

We know the story of Job and how the Lord allowed Satan to test him twice, but he was not able to take Job's life. I have read the book of Job in its entirety, and the Lord really allowed Satan to test Job, but he knew that Job would survive the tests, vicious as they were. All Satan can do in our lives is test us. Satan cannot do a thing unless the Lord allows him in our Holy Ghost-filled lives. There are times when the storms of life seem out of hand and again, having a bank full of prayer that we can draw interest on is essential.

People believe the same as I did, that the devil can destroy us. In 2006, during my medical storm, I was temporarily destroyed in my flesh and all but dead, but NOT in my Holy Ghost! Matthew 10:28, *"And fear not them which kill the body, but are not able to kill the soul: but rather fear him which is able to destroy both soul and body in hell."*

Hell is real and the soul will go to either Heaven or Hell.

We have a huge "victim" society today, or if you prefer a "blame game" world today. In my opinion, Satan brought in the full blame game we have. It is the wife's fault. No, it is the husband's fault. No, it is the cat's fault or maybe the dog's fault. The Lord is displeased with these situations. I heard a story once— actually it was a joke. A man said, "I did not kill that person. I promise he ran into that knife fourteen times." Really!

Satan is a very slick and wise serpent! II Corinthians 11:14-15, *"And no marvel; for Satan himself is transformed into an angel of light. Therefore it is no great thing if his ministers also be transformed as the ministers of righteousness; whose end shall be according to their works."*

So many times, in fiery prayer, I have received answers or warnings to be careful in certain areas of my life. Each one of us has our own Holy Ghost well and by the grace of God, I want to keep mine as clean as possible. So I ask myself, "Whose fault is it if I am lost?" I promise you, it is not Satan's fault for he has been overcome at Calvary. We have the Holy Ghost and should keep it lit with fiery prayer.

So, if something goes wrong in my life and I get mad, do not pray, skip church, or do not live right, Satan may have instigated the whole situation. I have to pray through my battles. Do not worry, the devil wants to smear our lives and he certainly can, but if we do not overcome (which we have the power to do), only we can keep ourselves out of Heaven—Satan cannot! So victory through the storm in Jesus' name!

Chapter 21
Raindrops from Heaven

I have spoken endlessly of the need for fiery, anointed prayer, but not much about weeping. Occasionally in prayer, I enter into a seemingly endless weeping spell. I remember a great song called "Tears Are a Language God Understands." Psalms 126:6 *"He that goeth forth and weepeth, bearing precious seed, shall doubtless come again with rejoicing, bringing his sheaves with him."*

In 2003, I received word that my mother had a heart attack. That was my mom and she lived her life with diet and exercise, so no way could my mom have a heart attack. She had a good outlook on life!

I heard about her heart attack on a Sunday after church. I was told she had walked around with chest pain for two days. It is a miracle she lived.

I cried, cried, and cried all of that Sunday afternoon, thinking she might not make it. Tears flowed and flowed. I had some selfish weeping mixed in with my burden for her because I loved her and did not want to lose her. This happened in November of 2003. What is amazing is the Lord had led me to fast ten days in October. No particular burden was involved in that fast. I knew the Lord probably wanted me to do that fast for His glory. I have often thought back to the weeping on the day of the heart attack and the fast a month earlier and I believe the Lord definitely intervened and gave Mom twelve more years to live!

At times when I weep, I definitely feel a cleansing. Back in the 1990s, while I was going through my lengthy depression, friends would tell me to purchase vitamin B-complex, which would help me cry out toxins. I purchased a great deal of B-complex and certainly did not shed any tears. Many folks would tell me it was easy for them to cry; others said they never wept. I put a real premium on the ability to cry and weep. Many times in the midst of fiery prayer, I would cry out to the Lord and then feel emotion to weep. We all have different experiences in Holy Ghost prayer.

I have spent time studying the book of Jeremiah, who was known as the weeping prophet. He lived in a very tough time and had been called at a young age by the Lord to prophesy to Israel. Jeremiah was greatly persecuted for his stand for the Lord. Much of his weeping was for sinners. He had little sign of results, but it was a great burden that he had. He still obeyed the Lord.

The great man of God, Verbal Bean, who I was honored to meet, wept much. I heard a story about Reverend Bean. He was seen sitting and weeping on a set of steps in a major city, while in much travail. Someone asked what he was doing and he answered with a question, "Has anyone wept over this city for the lost?" That remembrance has been planted in my mind!

I have occasionally wept for souls and have fervently called out many names of people that I would like to see receive the Holy Ghost. I promise weeping and travailing with a heavy burden will bring results. Sometimes the exact results I expect never seem to happen, but the Lord has recorded every prayer!

Chapter 22
Freedom-What is it?

When I reached the wished for age of twenty-one in 1968, my father, out of nowhere, handed me a massive stock portfolio. He had promised me three thousand dollars when I returned from being overseas in the military. All I had to do was stay off hard liquor. I was allowed to drink beer and wine, but nothing else, to earn that money.

Stupidly, I still became drunk as I could on beer and wine even though I wanted my three thousand dollars. Instead, as I mentioned, my father handed over that massive portfolio and walked out of the kitchen back to his office. Wow! I was rich! I could skip college and just go crazy. Wine, women, and song—I was now free to do whatever I wanted and, like a twenty-one year old with no responsibility, I did just that.

It took me about three years of my so-called new-found freedom to wind up in a mental institution. Where did my freedom that I cherished so much go? I eventually learned the pleasure of sin is but for a season. Thank the Lord for the brief season it was. I wound up on my deathbed with fear, anxiety, depression, and many suicidal thoughts. Not to blame my dad, but I did not get any education on what to do with this sum of money. After six to eight months, I was institutionalized and cared not whether I had a dime. Whatever freedom meant to me, it evaporated into a cloud of morbid mental anguish. I mean, I had it all (I thought), but I really had absolutely nothing.

Prior to my terrible experience with intense counseling, Dad all but made me go to college, which turned out to be a three day experience. I stayed semi-drunk the entire time. Then, out the back door of college I went and on to my early downhill life trend.

One night, in Philadelphia, my uncle Charlie came to see me. I will never, ever forget the words he prophetically told me. I really do not think he knew what he was saying, so I will say the Lord used him to say what he did. He said, "Ye shall know the truth and the truth shall set you free."

At the time, as I remember, the words were useless and wasted. For six more months, I endured the living hell of FAD as I call it—Fear, Anxiety, Depression, and torment of the mind. Anything that I called freedom was only a thought. I was drugged occasionally for anxiety. One time, I was locked up for three days and somewhat comatose from their overdose. I had a perfect vision of myself screaming in hell fire. Freedom was elusive. I barely lived through that event, but thank God I did. Hell was at my doorstep. I asked God if He existed. The whole situation was a disaster.

I had to have God if there was one. In February of 1971, I got permission to leave for a week and go to Denver to visit my sister Dottie, who was at Denver University at that time. I asked someone on the plane to Denver where we were going. With concern, someone asked me if I was okay. I had temporarily lost my sanity—very scary.

When I finally arrived in Denver, my sister picked up her one hundred fifty pound, glassy-eyed brother. There was no freedom. I did not even think about freedom.

After a week in Denver, while living on my drugs they gave me back at the institution, my sister told me a Pentecostal minister and his wife wanted to meet me. She had me to go upstairs in her apartment building and meet them. Uneventful and fearful as it was, they did talk me into going to church with their son and daughter-in-law. I went Sunday out of duty and was told about Acts 2:38 *"Then Peter said unto them, Repent, and be baptized every one of you in the name of Jesus Christ for the remission of sins, and ye shall receive the gift of the Holy Ghost."* It meant nothing to me and I did not care if I went back or not.

A week later, a friend invited me to a party with many pro-tennis players, who were in Denver for a tournament. I went to the party for five minutes. I told him I would die if I did not get to church and repent of my sins. The Lord intervened! I got to the house of the

Lord, repented, and got baptized in Jesus' name for the remission of my sins. A few months later, I received the Holy Ghost after much prayer. No one from the institution had plans to come after me two thousand miles away.

This Holy Ghost, with time and the prayer that fueled it, brought me peace. All material things meant nothing. Peace, peace, peace was, and is, the treasure. As the years went by, I began to remember the words of my uncle, "Ye shall know the truth and the truth shall make you free." Once again, it was fiery prayer and worship that fueled my Holy Ghost experience to absolute freedom and sanity. Lord Jesus, I say a great big thank you for the experience forty-six years ago. The truth has made me free from the mental grips of hell! Fiery, anointed prayer will keep you free.

Chapter 23
Oops, The Wrong Way!

I saw a film clip in the 1960s of one play in a football game I will never, ever forget. The short film strip had a kick-off and the player who caught the ball headed full speed ahead down the field. As usual, everybody went after the guy with the ball- nothing new here. He got hit by one player and had an attempted tackle by another. Still on his feet, he took a few more hits, but was able to stay on his feet. Amazing!

Then something happened. The guy got hit so many times that he got spun around and began running the wrong way. He was protected by the opposing team as his own team tried to tackle him. I remember four or five players on the opposing team defended him as he rushed in to his own end zone, giving his opponents a touchdown (a wrong way touchdown). It was as if his own team fought to stop him, but to no avail!

Life has many wrong way experiences. You should be going one way, but you wind up going the other way. So it is in this wonderful Truth of Acts 2:38. Many started in the right direction, but ceased to pray and got caught in the crosswinds of the wrong direction. If we stop praying, Satan can tear into us. Ephesians 6:16, *"Above all, taking the shield of faith wherewith ye shall be able to quench all the fiery darts of the wicked."* Ephesians 6:18, *"Praying always with all prayer and supplication in the Spirit, and watching thereunto with all perseverance and supplication for all saints."* Much anointed prayer, which I have followed daily for many years, will certainly keep one from going the wrong way.

I have met many people over the years that believe a little differently than they did originally. Just like that player—he sincerely thought he was going in the right direction even though he got turned around from the many hits he received.

Great and wonderful people can seem to be established in the Truth, but are then hit hard by friends with another doctrine; I have seen them get turned around and give into another belief system. I will promise you there was a time in my life when I almost got turned around, but through intensive prayer and seeking the Lord nightly, I survived.

In the Gospels, some fell from the faith. The one place I absolutely do not want to get turned around is in my salvation. Over many years, I have watched false doctrines pull good people away from the Lord, and they are plentiful!

As I said earlier, Satan cannot pull us out of a strong Holy Ghost filled church, but he can tempt us sorely. He will test our Holy Ghost space daily. James 4:7 *"Submit yourselves therefore to God. Resist the devil, and he will flee from you."* I find it much easier to resist the devil with a powerful, daily, anointed prayer life.

Many times, I have put blinders on or knocked off the rear-view mirror of my life to not look back and instead have gone forward when I got hit by the devil. So many times it would have been easy to have been destroyed by going the wrong way. I thank the Lord for a daily calling in prayer to protect my soul!

That football player was very sincere in scoring a touchdown for his team, but things can happen. Occasionally, I ask Bishop Holmes to let me know if he sees me going the wrong way in any area! Hebrews 13:17 *"Obey them that have the rule over you, and submit yourselves: for they watch for your souls, as they that must give account, that they may do it with joy, and not with grief: for that is unprofitable for you."* Thank God for this Scripture!

Chapter 24
Anchored to What?

     I remember, while I was in Denver, that I did a lot of bass fishing in a lake owned by some folks I taught tennis to. They always insisted I use the rowboat they kept at their boathouse. I was very thankful for this because they had a small anchor in the boat with about twenty feet of rope. When bass fishing, I would be in one place on the water and when a breeze came up, I just dropped the anchor and stayed in one place unless there were high winds. Of course, the anchor did not hold in those conditions.

     I have read about many ships at sea that were hit by storms, but because of an anchor thrown into the sea, the ship would remain in one place until the storm abated. Many stories have been told of the lives that would have been lost without an anchor to hold them in one place. A ship without an anchor in a storm would have been tossed to and fro until it sank.

     My son-in-law, Sammy, and I were fishing on a river in Arkansas when he threw the anchor out of the boat because we were moving too quickly. That boat stopped immediately when the anchor hit bottom. After fishing for a while, he went to pull the anchor up. He pulled and pulled and no anchor. With a closer look, he realized the anchor had landed in some tree branches under the water. After awhile we got the anchor pulled up. It was a mission!

Years ago a song came out called "I've Anchored My Soul in the Haven of Rest." Great song! Hebrews 6:19 *"Which hope we have as an anchor of the soul, both sure and stedfast…"*

I must be anchored to my faith in Jesus Christ and want to be anchored so strongly in prayer that Satan cannot pull the anchor loose. I think of the time spent fishing with Sammy. That anchor was all but stuck in that tree.

The winds and storms of life will rip and tear at our ship (soul), but if we are anchored solidly in Christ, we will make it to Heaven's shoreline.

Anointed prayer makes Christ so alive, as well as securing our anchor of salvation!

Chapter 25
Just a Little Nudge

By far, one of the most powerful teachings of Bishop Holmes is this, "listen to your nudges." When I first received the Holy Ghost, I was not a man of much prayer, but I did start feeling those little nudges from the Lord. I could feel a nudge in my soul. It was usually something that I did not want to do. In 1972, some relatives flew out to Steamboat Springs, Colorado. They came from Philadelphia and, of course, I lived in Denver, which was just three hours away. They were extremely excited about a real estate deal and wanted me to meet them in Steamboat, which I did.

The land was beautiful! They invested in the land and I bought two lots myself. A ski area was to be developed along with roads and other amenities. Before I made my down payment, there was a nudge of "I just do not know about this." I had the money and it had to be good. Later in the day, I looked up at the beautiful development to be and I had a firmer nudge of wishing I had not made this investment, but it just had to work!

Fast forward five years—I had been paying on it for five years and all of a sudden, I was being sued for the full payment of the land. Ouch! I retained an attorney to help me, but he proved to be useless. The farmers who owned the original land kept the promissory notes from day one in case the development company went bankrupt. Well, they did go bankrupt and after my attorney failed to get the farmer who sold to me to reduce his claim, I managed to get the price down on my own. Now I owned two beautiful lots that were completely undeveloped. I kept thinking a company would take over the land and develop it. Year after year went by. I paid taxes on it each year and in 1997, after almost thirty thousand dollars invested, I sold it for six thousand dollars before we moved to Little Rock.

Just a simple nudge and I could have told my relatives I am not going to invest. Just a simple nudge would have saved many headaches and thousands of dollars! Over many years in my comings and goings, the Lord has given me a nudge (and sometimes a strong one) to invite someone to church. Very rarely did I ignore a nudge to invite someone to church, but if I did, I can promise you I suffered into the night. We are here to be witnesses and I have learned to obey the Lord the best I can with those nudges to invite people to church.

One time, I was parked next to a lady at a convenience store. A definite nudge to invite her to church hit me. She looked angry and unkempt and I had my reasons not to invite her. Maybe she had a gun and would shoot me. I could not get out of this one. I can be stubborn. Well, I drove off knowing I was supposed to invite this lady. So I turned around and went back to the store knowing she would be gone. Not a chance, so I got a testimony and with a huge smile walked up to her car window. She was very thankful I gave her an invitation. I felt I had obeyed the Lord no matter what she said and was at peace. You may save a soul by listening to a nudge and there is nothing more important!

I could lay out other examples where I did not listen to a nudge, but that by far and away was the worst financial scenario. I will say, there was a great nudge in 1973 that, thank God, I followed, as strange as it was. I met my wife, Linda, in Starks, Louisiana in the late summer of 1973 and after a few minutes of talking to her, I was excited. She was told she could have nothing to do with me, but after talking with my Denver pastor, he told me to go get her if I felt that was the right thing to do. I had met many girls in Pentecost, but for marriage all were thumbs-down nudges.

To make a long story short, I called Linda, flew down to Texas and we met behind her workplace. We drove to Houston, flew right back to Denver and married a few weeks later. I will promise anyone if you have a nudge to not marry someone, pay attention. God moves in mysterious ways and that was certainly one of them.

Nudges, just little nudges, can lead to life and death situations and decisions!

My son and I have a great land business due to the Lord and Bishop Holmes being guided by Him.

Thank God my son wanted my involvement and what a blessing it has been. We never make a decision on land without prayer. Sometimes we feel great about a piece of land and the next day, we both will agree to make an offer or forget it. We put the Lord first in all we do.

Whatever in life the situation might be, the Lord will give a yes or no nudge after good prayer and maybe some fasting!

Chapter 26
Effort

I remember, in my youth, some teachers would say to me, "Well, you get an 'E' for effort." That was encouraging until I saw the grade. In other words, "Good try, but you need to get a passing grade." My effort levels were there one day and gone the next in regards to grades. However, my efforts in sports were intense and the rewards many times were great.

Bishop Holmes has spoken numerous times from the pulpit about how the Lord honors effort. In the last few years, I have really come to a revelation of effort—it does produce miracles! Bishop Holmes had told my son, Seth, "You may need to look at one hundred pieces of land to find one to buy." That was not uplifting to me five or six years ago; however, I have learned there is no wasted time in true effort. Almost daily, Seth, Bram, or Falon go with me to look at land and every now and then, we buy a property and we do very well with it! There was a time where I knew that most of what we looked at we would not buy. Now I am very excited to make the effort because of some great deals out there.

Four or five years ago, Seth wanted me to go to an auction with him. The night before we were to go, I got sick and Seth was slowly thinking about backing out, but as sick as I felt, I wanted us to go. The next morning, I awoke feeling all right and we went. The result was the right purchase and a piece of land that, to this day, is producing monthly payments.

God has ways of blessing our health if we make an effort to eat right. I learned a long time ago that eating poorly and going to an altar for prayer did not work out well. The Lord dealt with me to make some eating changes and, as a result, guess what? Better health.

Every day that goes by, I try to make an effort to pass out a small nutshell of my testimony. That is one effort I have a conviction for. There is a Heaven and a Hell and I want to do my best to get visitors. The best place for a visitor to be is in the fiery, anointed services in the house of the Lord!

Many times, while I am in prayer, Seth will text me, "Dad, we just sold another piece of land." I can promise you, it is an effort to get to prayer and then stay in prayer on some mornings or evenings, but the rewards of anointing are great! I have learned every effort for the Lord, whether it be outreach, financial, health, or spiritual, will be rewarded!

Chapter 27
Internet (the phone)

It is amazing how far technology has come in a very short time. I have learned that many dislike the internet while others love it. Little children that cannot even talk yet know how many times to punch a few buttons and find things. It seems almost innocent at times. Other people, myself included, struggle with the internet or hardly use it.

I remember television in the 1950s. We thought it was great—"Captain Kangaroo," "Roy Rogers" and on and on. But after a few years, it became problematic. I wanted to see a certain show, my sisters fought for their shows, and then my Dad would come into the room. That is when we all took a back seat to his choices such as "Gilligan's Island" and the "Beverly Hillbillies." Mom would make her voice heard when dinner was ready and I remember saying, "Mom, it will be over in five minutes. They have not caught the bad guy." The television did cause division in the home. We finally tried to solve the problem with a second TV. All I can say is that was double trouble.

Television came to America over a period from 1947-1957. I would say it was an amazing invention that brought devastation to the family unit! I think today most homes in America have multiple TVs. Bar and grill type restaurants have become popular because they offer ten or more televisions where people can watch multiple shows simultaneously.

At times, people will ask me if I have a TV and my answer is, "No." Years ago, when I told folks I had no television, they felt sorry for me. Now, many say, "Smart move" because it is so bad. Sorry to be graphic, but every home has a septic line going out to the street. For years, I have thought of the TV as a septic line coming into the home, which damages the heart and soul of America.

Now that our genius technology has advanced to the internet, phones, and all kinds of good and evil, I find it to be much more evil than good. We have to make our own decision to really serve the Lord. We are in a day (as Bishop Holmes has preached) that serving the Lord has to be in our heart!

I have never thought of my walk with the Lord as a "can do" or "cannot do" journey. I love my Lord so much that it is my desire to do right. I have a few news sites I read on my phone and I promise you that no matter where you go on that phone, there is some evil salted in everywhere! As Bishop Holmes preaches, God allowed the internet to find out what really is in everyone's heart. How true that is!

Anyone can go to a wicked site without Mom and Dad knowing, and Mom and Dad can do the same. So where does this once again bring me? Fiery, anointed prayer is my firewall against the trash of this world. We all carry these "trees" of good and evil in our pocket that can send us to one side of eternity or the other!

God help me stay in fiery prayer. The Lord is the only force, through anointing, that can save me!

Chapter 28
Pillar of Salt

When our great God delivers us out of a tough situation, I can promise you He does not want us looking back to where we came from. Just a peek back can anger Him. Out of the Lord's kindness and Abraham's prayers, the Lord delivered Lot and his family from the wicked cities of Sodom and Gomorrah before He cast fire and brimstone down from Heaven to destroy them. Genesis 19:15, *"And when the morning arose, then the angels hastened Lot, saying, Arise, take thy wife, and thy two daughters, which are here; lest thou be consumed in the iniquity of the city."*

As Lot and his family were leaving the city, the Lord spoke. Genesis 19:17, *"Escape for thy life; look not behind thee, neither stay thou in all the plain; escape to the mountain, lest thou be consumed."* But the Lord's anger arose in Genesis 19:26 *"But his wife looked back from behind him, and she became a pillar of salt."* There have been times in my life when I could have looked back on a certain situation, but it was with much prayer, convictions, and nudges that I was able to look forward.

A football player about to catch a pass has to look back to catch the ball, but then it is full speed ahead without looking back. Looking back slows his progress and, in professional football, one needs every one hundredth of a second to score. In a horse race, it is so critical that a horse run straight ahead, led by his rider, that he has blinders on to attain the first place prize.

Many people have a painful past, but the Lord wants to give them a new start. Yes, it does take time to move forward as it did in my case, but I was not going to look back. The past was on my mind, but I had absolutely no desire to return to it.

Hebrews 12:1 *"Wherefore seeing we also are compassed about with so great a cloud of witnesses, let us lay aside every weight, and the sin which doth so easily beset us, and let us run with patience the race that is set before us."*

I write this with a few temptations to look back, but I felt a heavy conviction to not even peek back, but to be as the racehorse with blinders on, and do my best to go forward. I can promise that an anointed, fiery prayer life will drive you forward. Actually, there are times when the Lord has really helped me let things go in great prayer. I desperately wanted to move forward in Christ, whereas Lot's wife was holding on to some things back in Sodom and Gomorrah. The results will be great in time. It does take a little patience, so I say "forward pray"! Do not look back, pull up yesterday's anchor, and move on.

Chapter 29
The Well is Pure

I began spending summer time at my grandma's camp in the beautiful Adirondacks when I was eight or nine years old. I had arrived at the same time that she did one summer when she took me down to an old rusty pump. My grandma instructed me to start lifting the pump handle up and down. I did so, but with very little enthusiasm. I was getting tired; however, she said to keep on pumping. I switched my hands more than a few times.

After a little while, I heard some gurgling in the well. Certainly no water in sight! This was getting me very tired and thirsty. Finally, some very dirty water with rust pieces in it dripped out. "Gross stuff," I thought. My grandma instructed me to keep going and I did. Eventually, lots of water was coming out, but it was still very dirty. Even though I was so exhausted, I kept pumping. The water began to clear up very slowly. She said, "We are getting there." Of course, I wondered where "getting there" was!

Finally, the water cleared up! Wow! It was cold and clear and believe me, I was very thirsty from all my hard work. My grandma pumped the handle so I could get a drink. Ice cold, delicious spring water was now flowing. It was wonderful! It took time and patience and, if my grandmother had not stood there pushing me, I would have quit before the first gurgle came from the well.

Jesus spoke in John 7: 37-39 "*If any man thirst, let him come unto me, and drink. He that believeth on me, as the scripture hath said, out of his belly shall flow rivers of living water. (But this spake he of the Spirit, which they that believe on him should receive: for the Holy Ghost was not yet given; because that Jesus was not yet glorified.)*"

I am sure everyone would like a drink of that ice cold water I got out of the well many years ago in the Adirondack mountains, but what has brought me to where I am today is what Jesus mentioned in John 7:38 regarding the living water. Many reading this book have received the Holy Ghost. Jesus referred to the Holy Ghost as living water, but is that living water still flowing in our lives? I have always thought of anointed prayer as the rivers of living water.

Every day and many nights I have a great thirst for this living water in prayer and I can promise you that sometimes you have to pump the handle, spiritually speaking, for a while to get all the junk out of your mind and heart from the day we live in. Patience and a clean heart will bring one into that wonderful living water!

Chapter 30
Enduring to the End

Endurance can be defined as the ability or the strength to continue or last, especially despite fatigue, stress, or other adverse conditions. I will say many times I endured in sports until the game was over, even though sometimes I had great thirst, frustration, and exhaustion. In my studies, I did not have a whole lot of endurance due to other interests; however, I got by.

My thoughts go to the greatest event folks will ever receive, recorded in Acts 2:38 *"Then Peter said unto them, Repent, and be baptized every one of you in the name of Jesus Christ for the remission of sins, and ye shall receive the gift of the Holy Ghost."* Getting the Holy Ghost is one great event and then fueling it with prayer is the other! Matthew 24:13 *" But he that shall endure to the end, the same shall be saved."*

Endurance to the end in anything can be very tough. The greatest endurance we face is for our salvation. Perilous times are now everywhere. Absolute evil is being called good. The bad guys seem to be the good guys and the people trying to do right (Christians) are the bad ones.

I think of all the ships that have met the end of their journey (especially when lighthouses were not plentiful) by smashing against the reefs, sand bars, or rocks as they reached the perilous shorelines. Ships were that close to the shorelines when real trouble came.

Many planes are fine once they are in the air, but there have been many bad landings over the years that have caused death and destruction. I have often heard on the radio about mishaps "when they were about to land." I have also heard in the news that something bad happened to an athlete "when he/she was about to cross the finish line."

Perhaps one of the most powerful Scriptures I mentioned early in this chapter is about enduring to the end to be saved. When the Lord melts the earth, all the halls of fame, all of man's accomplishments, and anything we might think will continue to exist in the earth will be gone. II Peter 3:10 *"But the day of the Lord will come as a thief in the night; in the which the heavens shall pass away with a great noise, and the elements shall melt with fervent heart, the earth also and the works that are therein shall be burned up."*

This is not what I think, but this is the Word of God.

All I know is that the soul of man will depart the body for a glorious Heaven or an eternal red-hot Hell. There is much discussion on this subject; however, I will finish this chapter with a Scripture referring to Lazarus and the rich man. Luke 16: 19-26: *" There was a certain rich man, which was clothed in purple and fine linen, and fared sumptuously every day: And there was a certain beggar named Lazarus, which was laid at his gate, full of sores, And desiring to be fed with the crumbs which fell from the rich man's table: moreover the dogs came and licked his sores. And it came to pass, that the beggar died, and was carried by the angels into Abraham's bosom: the rich man also died, and was buried; And in hell he lift up his eyes, being in torments, and seeth Abraham afar off, and Lazarus in his bosom. And he cried and said, Father Abraham, have mercy on me, and send Lazarus, that he may dip the tip of his finger in water, and cool my tongue; for I am tormented in this flame. But Abraham said, Son, remember that thou in thy lifetime receivedst thy good things, and likewise Lazarus evil things: but now he is comforted, and thou art tormented. And beside all this, between us and you there is a great gulf fixed: so that they which would pass from hence to you cannot; neither can they pass to us, that would come from thence."*

This Scripture defines almost an immediate trip to Heaven for Lazarus and indicates the rich man went to Hell. I want to make it clear that if you are rich and full of the Holy Ghost and live in anointed prayer you will endure the tough times to the end and be saved! As everyone knows, Christianity is under great persecution in the world today, even in America. The shoreline of eternity may be closer than we think.

Meet the Author

Photo credit: Ken Bourn

Seth Pomeroy lives in North Little Rock, Arkansas with his wife, Linda. He received the gift of the Holy Ghost forty-six years ago and is a member of the First Pentecostal Church of North Little Rock, Arkansas, where he wholeheartedly supports its leadership: Bishop J.N. Holmes and Pastor Nathan Holmes.

He and his wife have raised their three children, Sharon (Pomeroy) Townley, Kara (Pomeroy) Cypert and Seth T. Pomeroy, to love the Lord and to cultivate a prayer life. The benefits of this way of living shine forth through all of their children. He also owns Pomeroy Land Development, LLC along with his son, Seth T. Pomeroy.